Drama *Scripts*

To Julie and David

For performance rights please contact Roy McGregor c/o Hodder Gibson, 2a Christie Street, Paisley, PA1 1NB, tel: +44 (0) 141 848 1609, fax: +44 (0) 141 889 6315, email: hoddergibson@hodder.co.uk

Although every effort has been made to ensure that website addresses are correct at time of going to press, Hodder Gibson cannot be held responsible for the content of any website mentioned in this book. It is sometimes possible to find a relocated web page by typing in the address of the home page for a website in the URL window of your browser.

Orders: please contact Bookpoint Ltd, 130 Milton Park, Abingdon, Oxon OX14 4SB. Tel: +44 (0)1235 827720. Fax: +44 (0)1235 400454. Lines are open from 9.00–5.00, Monday to Saturday, with a 24-hour message answering service. Visit our website at www.hoddereducation.co.uk. Hodder Gibson can be contacted direct on: Tel: +44 (0)141 848 1609; Fax: +44 (0)141 889 6315; email: hoddergibson@hodder.co.uk

Impression number   10   9   8   7   6   5   4
Year   2010   2009   2008   2007

Typeset in Stone Sans 8/10pt by Fakenham Photosetting Limited
Printed and bound in Malta

A catalogue record for this title is available from the British Library

ISBN: 978-0-340-90466-4

Contents

Introduction to Pupils

What is the point of Drama? Hopefully you will find something that will entertain or amuse you within these three plays; they were written especially for young people. You will probably find the characters interesting, perhaps even likeable. When you read and perform the plays they will open up your imagination. If any (or all) of these things happen then that is a point of Drama. But there is more.

Drama can, if done properly, build your confidence and help your social and interpersonal skills. In fact it can change you as a person. For this to happen you will have to meet it half way. You will only get out of Drama what you're prepared to put into Drama. I hope that you get a lot out of these plays. It's why they were written.

Introduction to Teachers

These plays grew from what I felt was a lack of interesting new script material for teaching drama. Through a process of trial and error, each of them was created and revised – what didn't work in practice was taken out, and what did work was kept in. At this point I began to consider their use in the English curriculum. The English room is a different kettle of fish from the drama studio, and so the drafting process began again in order to find the right balance between practical drama work and the academic rigours of studying a play for English.

Of course, there are crossovers in both subjects, and these were my main focus. Both subjects have the idea of communication and understanding at their core. Through reading and analysis we can appreciate and enjoy a text more, regardless of which discipline we are working within.

Although there is a large cast list in the three plays, there are opportunities for double casting. Some characters have a more demanding role than others, although I would hold that each is equally important: *There are no small parts, just small actors*. Class sizes will also have an effect on working with the plays. I would suggest that if you have a relatively small class, and double casting doesn't solve the problem, then feel free to try merging the lines of one character with another. I would hope that this is a last resort!

The tasks provide opportunities for individual as well as group work, both oral and written. These are points that should not be ignored by the Drama teacher. Time should be allowed for the student of both English and Drama to analyse the story, characters and structure of the plays.

Finally, I would like to emphasise that these plays are not fixed and 'untouchable'. I want them to be flexible enough to stretch pupils across a wide range of abilities. Teachers can encourage pupils to be experimental, taking away scenes or indeed creating new scenes if they wish. In short, feel free to do a bit of *stitching* of your own!

Roy McGregor

Diagram of stage directions

USR	USC	USL
CSR	CS	CSL
DSR	DSC	DSL

↑ **audience** ↑

USR upstage right   **USC** upstage centre   **USL** upstage left

CSR centrestage right   **CS** centrestage   **CSL** centrestage left

DSR downstage right   **DSC** downstage centre   **DSL** downstage left

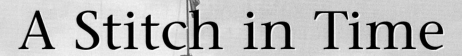

A Stitch in Time

by

Roy McGregor

ACT ONE
SCENE ONE Tent Day

Blackness. Western movie theme playing loud. Sound of guns and shouting. Everything gets louder until the lights are snapped on and then immediate silence. We are in a tent with a table CS. On the table is a crystal ball. Under the table is a figure crouching over, covering himself with his arms. He looks terrified. A door opens CSR and JIMMY enters slowly.

JIMMY: Hello?

Pause.

JIMMY: Hello?

JIMMY goes over to the figure and taps him on the arm.

JIMMY: Hello?

The figure looks up at JIMMY and screams in fear and runs off. JIMMY is obviously quite frightened by this and starts to creep slowly towards the exit. He gets to pull back the curtain when the figure appears again, this time confident and in charge. The figure is MEPHIS.

MEPHIS: Hello, boy! Mephis the Magnificent. How can I be of service?

JIMMY: Eh, hello. I just came in to...

MEPHIS: To what? You realise you just saved my bacon?

JIMMY: What do you mean?

MEPHIS: One-eyed Jack and his gang had me dead for rights.

JIMMY: Who's One-eyed Jack?

MEPHIS: Why the toughest, meanest, black hearted, pig-sucking scum that ever walked this earth. I hope that he didn't see you.

JIMMY: See me? When?

MEPHIS: When? Why just there. When you came in. You certainly gave me a scare. Anyway, what can I do for you?

JIMMY: I'm here about the job. It said Saturdays and Sundays. I need the extra money for the holidays.

MEPHIS: You ever worked in the carnival before? And do you know anything about the old crystal ball?

JIMMY: I was told that it was just general duties. Cleaning up and the like.

MEPHIS bursts out laughing.

MEPHIS: Good thing it's not the elephant tent, eh?

The door opens and CUSTOMER enters.

CUSTOMER *(nervously)*: I was in earlier.

MEPHIS: You were indeed, my friend. Well, have you decided?

CUSTOMER: Yes, I want to go through.

MEPHIS: On your head be it. But remember not to jump too far.

CUSTOMER: Yes. I promise I'll be careful.

MEPHIS: You can go back there and... well, change your life.

CUSTOMER: I understand.

The CUSTOMER exits USC.

MEPHIS *(shouting)*: Wait, you don't have a timepiece! Oh, well... He'll soon realise. How do you calculate the time without a timepiece?

JIMMY: Well, can I get the job? I won't let you down. I'll never be late. I'm very polite.

MEPHIS: Oh yes, you've got the job, but can I tell you something, Jimmy? You must never, ever, ever, ever, ever, ever, *(shouting)* EVER!!! PLAY WITH THE CRYSTAL BALL OR EXPLORE ON YOUR OWN!!!

JIMMY: Okay, cool it!

MEPHIS *(calmly)*: Fine. You have the job. Start Saturday. My name is Mr Mephis.

In the background we can hear very slightly shouts and screams. This grows as the scene continues.

JIMMY: But what do I do?

MEPHIS: You just keep a record of who goes in and who comes out.

An old woman, MRS CULPEPPER, *appears with a brush and starts to sweep up.*

MRS CULPEPPER: The curtain has moved, Mr Mephis.

MEPHIS: Eh, yes, Mrs Culpepper... We have a... client?

MRS CULPEPPER *(knowingly)*: I quite understand, sir.

She exits.

MEPHIS: Right, well now there then, I'll have to be going myself. You can see yourself out?

JIMMY: Sure... Here, how did you know my name? And what is there to explore? It's only a tent.

MEPHIS *leaves CSR.*

JIMMY *stands and looks about. The lights go down until the tent is awash with green and red.*

The sound of screaming and shouting slowly comes up from the background. It gets louder and louder. As it does so JIMMY *looks more frightened. The curtain where the* CUSTOMER *went, USC, starts to shake.* JIMMY *exits where he entered, CSR. The sound gets louder.*

Suddenly the CUSTOMER, *partly dressed as a pirate, runs out. He runs down to CS exhausted. He looks terrified.*

CUSTOMER: I went too far! I didn't have a timepiece! Help me!

A group of PIRATES *come screaming out from behind the curtain of USC. They are carrying knives and pistols. They grab the* CUSTOMER *and drag him screaming behind the curtain.*

The noise subsides as the lights go down slowly to blackout.

SCENE TWO Living room Night

DAVID *and* ELSPETH MORRISON *are waiting for their son,* JIMMY, *returning home.* DAVID *is standing at the window.* ELSPETH *is sitting on a chair with a cup of tea.*

DAVID: Jimmy? Where are you? *(To Elspeth)* What time is it?

ELSPETH: Don't get onto him, David. He's having problems. It's called teenage angst. I read about it in a magazine. He'll be all right. Remember how you were at that age?

DAVID: Aye but I don't want that for my son, Elspeth. I want better for him. What father doesn't?

ELSPETH: You're driving him away from you with all your nagging. I know you're only trying to do your best, but he might not see it like that. Try and listen to him a bit more.

DAVID: Listen to him? He doesn't talk a language known to man nor beast. He mumbles all the time. He shuffles about the house like a wild animal. I can't say anything without him snapping at me.

ELSPETH: It's a phase he's going through.

DAVID: It's the window he'll be going through if there's any more cheek. *(Looking out of the window)* Is that him? No, it's just a dog. I'm telling you, Elspeth, he's got to buck up his ideas. At his age I had an after school job delivering papers, and a Saturday morning job on the milk round.

ELSPETH: Aye, aye, aye... you had to get up an hour before you went to bed. *(She laughs.)*

DAVID: You may laugh, but it's this attitude these days.

ELSPETH: You know who you sound like?

DAVID: Who?

ELSPETH: Your dad.

DAVID: Aye, maybe… I'm just concerned.

ELSPETH: I know that… I know that.

SCENE THREE Street corner Night

JIMMY *and* JENNIFER *stand talking to each other.*

JENNIFER: We'd better get going. It's late. My parents will be worried. What about yours?

JIMMY: Oh, mine will be fine. I can stay out all night if I want.

JENNIFER: Sure.

JIMMY: Do you want to go out on Saturday night?

JENNIFER: What about your new job? Down at that carnival, that sounds like fun. I'm not sure about Mephis the Magnificent, though. People are saying there's something strange about him. What's that all about on his poster – *You change the past, you change the future*?

JIMMY: He's all right really. A bit eccentric, maybe. That's all. Well, it finishes at six. Why don't you come down and meet me and we can go from there? Just tell them at the gate that you've to meet me and you won't have to pay in. We can have a free night at the carnival.

The lights go down and the stage then sparkles with lights, as if stars are dancing. A slow piece of music plays.

JIMMY and JENNIFER hold each other and dance romantically around the stage.

JENNIFER'S SONG

The colour of your eyes
The colour of your hair
The way you speak my name
Whenever you are there
The moon up in the sky
The stars and how they shine
They look down on our love
On this summer's night
The meaning's very clear
Whenever you are near
Jennifer...
Jennifer...

The music fades and then there is the sound of a car horn.

JENNIFER: That's my dad, I'd better go. I'll come by the carnival on Saturday.

She exits USR.

UNGER *enters from USL.*

UNGER: What you up to, you creep?

JIMMY: Oh, it's you Barry. Nothing. I was just going home.

UNGER: Any money?

JIMMY: I'm skint.

UNGER *(twisting* JIMMY'S *arm)*: The trouble with this town is that people are too poor. How is an enterprising young lad like myself supposed to extort money from the scabby headed populace when they go about like paupers? What's your dad do?

JIMMY: He was made redundant.

JIMMY is now on the ground with BARRY'S *foot on his back.*

UNGER: Redundant? That means he must have been rubbish at his job.

JIMMY: He wasn't rubbish at his job. They laid off a lot of people at the factory.

UNGER: Don't contradict me, you piece of muck.

JIMMY: I'm not muck.

UNGER: But you're at the bottom of my shoe. That's where muck usually gathers. Listen, I need money for the weekend so I want you to steal a few coppers out of your ma's purse. Your dad's wallet is probably full of moths. So you get me money, or else. Okay?

JIMMY: Okay, okay.

UNGER exits, USR, laughing.

Lights go down to a single spot on JIMMY, *CS.*

JIMMY *(to audience)*: That was Barry Unger… He's a moron… but he's bigger than me, so I do what I'm told. You get people like that all over. They're just bullies. I know, we're supposed to stand up to them, but that's easier said than done. He takes money from everybody in the school. Everybody's scared. A teacher told us that we should feel sorry for bullies. I don't feel sorry for him. I wish somebody would kick his face in.

DAVID *(voice offstage)*: Jimmy!! Jimmy!!

JIMMY: Gawd! It's my dad! I wish he didn't do that. Shouting out the window as if I'm five years old. *(Shouting)* Coming! *(To audience)* And here comes the big argument.

JIMMY runs off, CSL, shouting.

I've got a job! I've got a job! I've got a job!

SCENE FOUR Tent Night

MEPHIS *sits at table doing his books. He yawns, takes off his glasses and rubs his eyes.*

MEPHIS: It is so difficult a task I have been given, my father. The responsibility is great. How can I keep in order chaos? How long can I stave off its reign? The days are long and my time on this earth is short. Vita et mors.

A ROMAN CENTURION *appears from USC. He walks slowly downstage looking frightened. He is looking about. He sees* MEPHIS.

ROMAN CENTURION: Quis hic locus, quae regio, quae mundi plagi? Ubi sum? Sub ortu solis, an sub cardine glacialis ursae.*

MEPHIS (*softly*): You are in the wrong place, my friend. Return.

The ROMAN CENTURION *turns and walks back upstage and exits.*

And so they come. Sad spectres in search of their home. Imagine the horror of being lost from your time? It would be worse than death.

MRS CULPEPPER *breezes in from DSL.*

MRS CULPEPPER: Is that you talking to yourself again, you old fool? You ought to watch out or they'll be carting you off. I had an auntie who talked to herself. Said she saw figures. Figures? I ask you.

She puts on her coat.

Well, that's me. Another day over. Another day done. Another step towards the grave. (*She sighs*) Vita et mors, eh Mr Mephis? Life and death. It's what it's all about.

The sound of western music starts to creep in.

*(What place is this, what region, what quarter of the world? Where am I? Under the rising sun or beneath the wheeling course of the frozen bear?)

I'll be back Monday morning 8.30 on the dot. That's if I can lug these old bones out of my scratcher.

The music gets louder.

Screams.

MRS CULPEPPER: What the...

A group of about six COWBOYS *burst in from USC. They are screaming and waving guns about.*

Freeze.

Blackout.

Silence.

There will now be four tableaux. Between each tableau there is a blackout.

TABLEAU 1

COWBOYS pointing guns at MEPHIS *and* MRS CULPEPPER. MRS CULPEPPER *is hiding, cowering behind* MEPHIS *who is holding a chair threateningly.*

TABLEAU 2

MEPHIS *lying on the floor, the chair lying beside him.* MRS CULPEPPER *has her hand in the air. She is on the floor trying to ward off the looming* COWBOYS.

TABLEAU 3

MRS CULPEPPER *on her feet fighting with the* COWBOYS *who have grabbed her.*

TABLEAU 4

COWBOYS *dragging* MRS CULPEPPER *out, USC.* MEPHIS *on his feet reaching out.*

SCENE FIVE School Playground Day

JIMMY *stands around talking to some* FRIENDS.

JIMMY: So it's dead strange. This strange guy and the place is pure creepy. There's funny sounds.

FRIEND 1: What do you mean?

JIMMY: I don't know. Sort of whooping sounds and screaming.

They all laugh.

JIMMY: No, really. It's a weird place.

FRIEND 2: So why do you want to work there?

JIMMY: I don't really but… well, my dad's been going bonkers about me not doing enough and always asking for money.

DAVID *(voice offstage)*: What do you mean then? I give you money all the time.

The lights go down very slowly.

JIMMY: Last night was terrible.

FRIEND 3: Why? What happened?

Lights come up slowly, USR, as they go down CS.

JIMMY: Well, they were there when I got home.

JIMMY *walks into* FLASHBACK 1.

DAVID *is standing and* ELSPETH *is sitting in a chair, knitting.*

DAVID: So where have you been? Your mother and I have been sick with worry.

JIMMY: I was just talking to people.

ELSPETH: People? What people? I told you not to talk to strangers. There's too many funny folk around. Nobody's safe these days. Was a time you could walk about and feel safe. Those days have gone. You've got to be careful.

DAVID: Your mother's right, what with all these knives and guns on the street. I don't know what's happening to the world.

JIMMY: I was talking to a friend.

DAVID: What friend?

JIMMY *(embarrassed)*: Oh, come on, Dad.

ELSPETH: David, I think that he's talking about a girl.

DAVID: A girl? Oh, well, that puts a different light on it.

JIMMY: I didn't say it was a girl.

DAVID: Well, a boy of your age... I mean it's only natural, son.

JIMMY: I said it wasn't a girl. I went for a job interview.

ELSPETH *(standing)*: A job interview?

> *Lights go down on this and come up CS.*

FRIEND 1: Parents are always like that.

FRIEND 2: Yeah, totally embarrassing.

> JIMMY *walks downstage towards them.*

JIMMY: So I told them about my job and they seemed happy.

FRIEND 3: Do you think parents are human? Maybe there's something they're not telling us.

> BARRY UNGER *approaches from USL.*

JIMMY: Oh no, it's Unger.

FRIEND 2: Hide yer money and yer sweets.

UNGER: How's it going, scabby boys?

FRIEND 1: What do you want, Barry?

UNGER: I want your money and sweets.

FRIEND 1: Fair enough.

> *He gives him his money and sweets.*

> UNGER *notices* JIMMY.

UNGER: Heh, scabby boy! We keep running into each other. Get into yer ma's purse?

JIMMY: Not yet.

UNGER: Not yet? What is wrong with you people? *(Grabs* JIMMY *tightly by the lapels.)* You, son, are walking my streets. You are breathing my air. You are crossing my bridges. And, son, there is a toll to pay. When? Whenever I say.

JIMMY *looks to his friends for help.*

FRIEND 1 *walks up to* UNGER. UNGER *pokes him in the eye.*

FRIEND 1 *(staggering back in pain)*: My eye! My eye!

UNGER *faces them all, fists clenched.*

UNGER: You want it? All of you! You want it now? I'm the baddie here. Read it in your comics; watch it in your films. Look at me the wrong way and I'll punch your lights out. Ignore me and I'll punch your lights out. Try to take the mickey and I'll put you in your grave. All of you listen closely. Bring me money by the end of the week or I'll do you all. Understand?

ALL *(sheepishly)*: Aye, Barry. We understand...

UNGER *(turning to* JIMMY*)*: Now for you. *(He knees* JIMMY *in the groin.* JIMMY *falls to the ground.)*

Bell rings.

Good thing that bell rung or you would be dead.

UNGER *exits USL.*

JIMMY: You're a minger, Unger.

UNGER *(voice offstage)*: I heard that!

JIMMY: Sorry, Barry!

SCENE SIX Tent Morning

MEPHIS picks up the crystal ball that lies on the floor. He polishes it with a cloth and puts it back on the centre of the table. He is talking while doing so. We can see that he has a black eye and some cuts and bruising.

UNGER enters unseen. He hides behind a chest.

MEPHIS: It cannot go on. It cannot go on. Everyday they are getting closer. If they break through for good the world is in ruins. I will need to step through and reshape time. The bend has become too great. And what of that tear? No, things have to be sewn up. If this gets any worse dimension stepping will be as easy as hopping on and off a bus.

The trouble is that the Great Universe needs to be upgraded. But can I do this myself? I cannot. (*Looking up.*) Do you hear me? I cannot do this alone. What I need is the assistance of someone young and brave who can clear a pathway for me to work in peace. But where can I find such a one?

JIMMY breezes in.

JIMMY: Hi, Mr Mephis!

MEPHIS: Ah, Jimmy. You have answered my prayers.

JIMMY: Always glad to help.

MEPHIS: Listen, do you like travel?

JIMMY: I went to Spain once with my parents. That was cool.

MEPHIS: We can never rely on the weather. Anyway, where I'm thinking of is a lot further than Spain.

JIMMY: Is the carnival moving on?

MEPHIS: Let me tell you, one part of it wants to. One part of it is tired. One part of it needs rest. Do you like adventure?

JIMMY: I don't know what you mean.

MEPHIS: Do you crave excitement in your life?

JIMMY: With the threat of Barry Unger battering me, my life is pretty adventurous at the moment.

UNGER *sniggers.*

JIMMY *(looking around)*: What was that?

MEPHIS: Probably people outside the tent. We're never alone. Who is this Barry Unger?

JIMMY: Oh, just the school bully.

MEPHIS: Get me his address. I can arrange for one of my many friends to pay him a visit.

JIMMY: Thanks Mr Mephis, but I think that I'm going to have to stand up to him myself.

UNGER *nods his head sarcastically.*

MEPHIS: Sit down beside me. I have a story to tell you.

JIMMY *sits at a table with* MEPHIS.

The lights go down to a spot.

MEPHIS: I'm a very old man. I'm older than your father and a lot older than your grandfather. I have seen many things in my long life. Things that would amaze you and make you question your own eyes. A long time ago I met a man as old as myself now and he told me something that would change my life forever.

JIMMY: What did he tell you?

MEPHIS: He told me that monsters do not exist... and then he led me to their den.

JIMMY *(wide-eyed)*: Monsters?

MEPHIS: There are many things that we think exist only in the imagination, but are all too real. In this world within worlds we become like them. Stardust, nothing more. I am a protector, a guardian, whatever you want to call it.

JIMMY: What do you protect us from?

MEPHIS: You are not listening. There are forces that will try to destroy us. They want to enter our world.

JIMMY: But how can they do that?

MEPHIS *(pointing)*: Through that curtain, my young friend.

> JIMMY *gets up slowly and goes upstage to the curtain. He walks slowly, afraid.*

JIMMY: Here?

MEPHIS: A thousand years in a moment, a moment in a thousand years.

JIMMY: Cool. Can I go through?

MEPHIS: Why do the young want to rush towards death? We will go together, for I have a repair to do.

JIMMY: What sort of repair?

MEPHIS: There is a slight tear in time. I must get my needle and thread and mend it.

JIMMY: Wwwhoah, there, old man. What do you mean a tear in time?

MEPHIS: Imagine time as an object, a piece of material. It separates us from the past. This is how things must be, how they have always been. But time has been damaged. It happens now and again. It's no one's fault. But there are those who take advantage of this damage and step through to create havoc. They must be contained, for all of our sakes. Do you understand?

JIMMY: Clear as mud.

MEPHIS: Be patient. It will get clearer. I will go get the stuff I need. Meanwhile, go into that chest and pick a costume from the mid-nineteenth century United States.

JIMMY: A what?

MEPHIS: A cowboy outfit.

> MEPHIS *exits USR.*

> JENNIFER *enters USL.*

JENNIFER: Jimmy? Jimmy?

JIMMY: Jennifer? What are you doing here?

JIMMY goes USL. As he does so BARRY UNGER runs over to the table and hides under it.

JENNIFER: I've come to warn you. Barry Unger is looking for you and he knows where you're working. You've got to hide.

JIMMY: I'm not afraid of Barry Unger.

JENNIFER: Of course you are.

JIMMY: You're right, I am. But I'm going somewhere that he can't follow.

JENNIFER: Where's that?

JIMMY: It's a secret.

MEPHIS enters carrying a cowboy hat. He puts it on carefully.

MEPHIS: So this is your girlfriend?

JIMMY: How did you know that?

MEPHIS: I know everything.

JIMMY: Can she come with us?

MEPHIS: Jennifer, my dear, do you want to travel through space and time and meet strange and dangerous individuals?

JENNIFER: Cool. How did you know my name?

MEPHIS: Didn't you hear? I know everything. Now go into that chest and grab something to wear. We don't want to be conspicuous.

They open up the chest and look in amazed.

JENNIFER: Wow! This is impressive.

JENNIFER grabs a cowboy hat and a shawl and puts them on.

JIMMY: Get an eyeful of this, Jennifer!

He pulls out a holster without the guns and puts it on.

Where are the guns?

MEPHIS: Are you mad? One shot from you would send civilisation back a million years. And believe me, that was a bad time.

JIMMY: Sorry, Mr Mephis.

MEPHIS: Join hands.

They all join hands and turn their backs to the audience.

After three.

TOGETHER: One...

JENNIFER: No, I can't! I'm scared!

She runs towards exit.

JIMMY: Jennifer! Come back!

She exits.

MEPHIS: Leave her, Jimmy. We have work. One... two... three!

They rush towards the curtain, USC, and jump through it. There is a huge bang and a flash. They disappear.

UNGER comes from under the table.

UNGER *(to audience)*: He can run but he can't hide. *(Looking through the chest)* Now let's see what we have here. Okay there doesn't seem to be cowboy stuff. Ah, this'll do.

He pulls out a pirate hat and shoves it on quickly.

So that little prat is going to stand up to Barry Unger? I'll break his scrawny neck. Right, here we go. One... two... three!!!

He rushes towards the curtain just as JIMMY'S friends arrive.

FRIEND 1: Barry?

UNGER turns as he jumps through the curtain. He screams. There is a bang and a flash.

TOGETHER *(shocked)*: What on earth...!?!

END OF ACT 1

ACT TWO

SCENE ONE Happy Coconut Day

CAPTAIN BLACK DOG stands apart from the pirate crew overlooking their work. JAKE, PEG LEG, ONE-EYED TOM, QUELCH and BILLY FLOWERS are swabbing the deck. JOHN 'rip your guts out' ROE is doing a nice bit of polishing. Life on deck is lazy, relaxing, boring even?

Other DECK HANDS are going about deck business, keeping the place ship shape.

CAPTAIN BLACK DOG: Go to it lads. Let's keep this ship sparkling like the teeth of a South Sea Princess. We will raise the Jolly Rouge and sail all the seas of this world. Lads, we are invincible. Mr Flowers!

BILLY FLOWERS *(running up)*: Captain?

CAPTAIN BLACK DOG: Billy, me old friend. Inspect the decks.

BILLY FLOWERS: Aye, Captain.

BILLY FLOWERS starts to inspect the decks. He peers at stains and shakes his head. He approaches CAPTAIN BLACK DOG and whispers in his ear. He points at QUELCH.

CAPTAIN BLACK DOG: Quelch?

QUELCH *(standing up, sheepish)*: Aye, Captain?

CAPTAIN BLACK DOG: Quelch, my boy. There seems to be a mark on the deck of The Happy Coconut. It would appear to be a bloodstain.

QUELCH: Indeed it is Captain. I'm finding it difficult to remove the results of our blood-soaked lifestyle. It is a small mark though, Captain.

CAPTAIN BLACK DOG: No, lad, it is a large bloodstain.

QUELCH: No, Captain, I can assure you...

In one movement CAPTAIN BLACK DOG *has removed a pistol from his belt and let off a shot that rips through* QUELCH'S *leg. He falls to the deck screaming in agony.*

CAPTAIN BLACK DOG *(precisely)*: No, lad, I can assure you that it is a large bloodstain. John Roe and Billy Flowers! Throw that scurvy insolent dog down into quarters.

PEG LEG *(offering his crutch)*: Here, Quelch. Would ye like a loan of me crutch?

All the PIRATES *laugh.*

QUELCH *is carried below decks.*

CAPTAIN BLACK DOG: My trusty boys. I'm going to show you wonders of another world. But I need your cooperation. I need your loyalty. I need hard work. And I need you to be prepared to fight. Can ye do that?

ALL: Aye, Captain Black Dog!

ONE-EYED TOM: How can ye show us wonders of another world, Captain? For sure I thought this be the only world.

CAPTAIN BLACK DOG: That's where you're wrong, One-eyed Tom. The great universe stretches far beyond these lands we call home. Sometimes, though, there be holes in this eternal curtain.

ONE-EYED TOM: Holes, Captain?

CAPTAIN BLACK DOG: Aye, Tom. Holes like in a cheese. And lads, there be such a one here.

He picks up a map and points to a land mass.

And that's where we're headed. Now, lads, The Pirate Song. One, two, three –

THE PIRATE SONG

Chorus

ALL: The seas at our toes
The wind at our nose
We'll follow fortune
Wherever she goes

ONE-EYED TOM: My name is Tom Toon
I peeked out too soon
The lead took my eyeball
Right up to the moon!

ALL: CHORUS

JAKE: My name it is Jake
I'm a bit of a rake
A plank I will walk
If there's rum in that lake!

ALL: CHORUS

PEG LEG: They call me Peg Leg
'Cos the other leg is dead
It was buried at sea
And a prayer it was said!

ALL: CHORUS

BILLY FLOWERS: Billy Flowers that's me
I roam the high sea
Searching for treasure
A rich man I'll be!

ALL: CHORUS

QUELCH *(voice offstage)*: Jim Quelch now I am
My leg looks like jam
I'm bleeding to death
A priest or I'm damned!

ALL: CHORUS

CAPTAIN BLACK DOG (*slowly*): The pirate's life is rough
You've got to be tough
Or mutiny will stand
So come lend a hand
The Happy Coconut is sound
When trouble's around
You can join our little gang
Grab a pistol! Bang, bang!

ALL: CHORUS

The PIRATES *all go back to work.*

CAPTAIN BLACK DOG: Not long, lads. We're sailing to hell. Be happy!

CAPTAIN *laughs.*

SCENE TWO   Dodge City   Day

The stage is in darkness. The sound of a piano playing a saloon tune. The lights come up slowly. We are in a western saloon.

KITTY is tidying up tables and behind the bar. She walks downstage centre. The music fades.

KITTY: This is my saloon. It's a tough house, but a fair house. We get some scum-sucking pigs come in here trying to shoot the place up. That usually happens on payday at the Big Country Ranch. That's today, by the way, so if you ain't got a nose for trouble I'd suggest you vamoosh. Elam and Annie don't take kindly to strangers. My name's Kitty and you're in Kitty's Golden Nugget Saloon, in case you didn't know. You can drink my whisky, but don't go cursing, or I'll shoot you down like the dog you are.

She exits CSR.

A flash and a bang from USC and JIMMY *and* MEPHIS *come flying on.*

JIMMY: I think I'm going to be sick!

MEPHIS: Me first!

He grabs a spittoon and vomits into it.

JIMMY: Here, Mr Mephis, is that torn curtain the hole you're looking for?

He points to the curtain USC.

MEPHIS: Wait a minute, Jimmy. I've got to get rid of the chewy bits!

He vomits again.

KITTY *enters from CSR*

KITTY: Howdy strangers! First customers of the day. What'll it be?

JIMMY: I'll have a can of orange.

KITTY: You're not from around these parts. We drink whisky here. Whisky and more whisky. And if you can't do that I'll shoot you down like the dog you are.

JIMMY: I think I'll have a whisky then.

MEPHIS: I'll have a cup of tea, Kitty.

KITTY: How'd you know that my name is Kitty?

MEPHIS: I bin here before.

KITTY: It's a wise man that knows his past.

MEPHIS: And a wiser man that knows his future.

KITTY *(laughing)*: Hey old man, I like you! I'll git you that cup of tea.

She exits CSR.

MEPHIS: Right, Jimmy, to work.

JIMMY: First I'll clear my throat.

JIMMY *throws back the whisky.*

He starts choking.

MEPHIS: Be careful of the Red Eye. High-octane hootch, Jimmy. Right.

He goes into his bag and gets out the giant needle and thread. He threads it.

An art I learned at my mother's knee.

JIMMY: Did she sew for a living?

MEPHIS: No, no, she was a papyrus maker by the banks of the Nile.

MEPHIS *goes USC and looks at the torn curtain.*

JIMMY: Can you fix it?

MEPHIS: There's nothing Mephis can't fix. *(Thinking)* Well, there's only one thing Mephis can't fix.

ELAM KELLY *dressed in black enters from CSL.*

JIMMY: What can't you fix?

KELLY: Yeah, Mephis, just what can't you fix?

MEPHIS *(afraid)*: Oh no, it's Elam Kelly! There's only one thing worse than Elam Kelly.

JIMMY: What's that?

MEPHIS: Elam Kelly and Annie Mantee.

Enter ANNIE MANTEE.

MEPHIS: Oh no, it's Annie Mantee!

ANNIE: Howdy, pardners!

MEPHIS: There's only one thing worse than Annie Mantee and Elam Kelly.

JIMMY: What's that?

MEPHIS: That's Annie Mantee, Elam Kelly and their gang.

Enter the KELLY/MANTEE *gang. During the song there should be a wild dance.*

COWBOY SONG

Chorus

ALL: Welcome to the wild and woolly west
Think of yourself as a guest.
The buffalo are friendly
The injuns too.
The stars come out just for you.

ANNIE: My name is Annie, I'm a tough kinda gal
My father disowned me, I ain't got a pal.
But deep down inside, if truth be told
My little girl's heart is made out of gold

ALL: CHORUS

ELAM: My name is Elam, I know what you think.
I'll be dead if any more Red Eye I drink.
But under the earth I won't have my fill
If you visit bring a bottle right up to Boot Hill.

ALL: CHORUS

ONE-EYED JACK: Yo de diddle, yo de diddle di.
I'm going to heaven before I die.
I see my maker at the bottom of a cup.
I see the devil whenever I look up.

ALL: CHORUS ×2.

Slow repeat of last line

…just for yoooooooooo!

This should end in a howling from ALL.

MEPHIS: Change your underpants, Jimmy. This could be scary
buttons. Why howdy dowdy there, Annie. Long time no see.

ANNIE: Have we met before?

MEPHIS: Before and since.

ANNIE: What the hell does that mean?

MEPHIS: Annie, you're going to die in a pool of blood, face down in a gutter.

ANNIE pulls her gun.

ANNIE: Maybe you're going to die first.

MEPHIS: Historically that's not really possible.

KELLY: Maybe you shouldn't shoot the old man, Annie. Maybe you should shoot the coyote standing next to him.

JIMMY: Does he mean me?

KITTY enters with a cup of tea. She sees what's happening and puts the tea on the bar top. She reaches underneath the bar and pulls out a shotgun.

KITTY: You boys don't intend messin' up my nice saloon, do ya?

ANNIE: Certainly not Miss Kitty.

KITTY: Glad to hear it, Annie. Now if you'd like to put away those shooters and allow a gal to get a bit of peace it sure would be appreciated.

One of the gang comes up behind KITTY and points a gun to her head.

ANNIE: And if you'd like to put that gun down maybe my boy won't blow your head clean off. Boys, lock these critters in the cellar. We'll decide what to do with them later.

KITTY, MEPHIS and JIMMY are rounded up and taken off CSR.

ANNIE: Crack open the whisky, boys. Let's get some more music, dancin' and mayhem going. This is gonna be a wild party!

They all whoop, scream and cheer.

SCENE THREE Living Room Night

DAVID *is sitting on the couch while* ELSPETH *paces up and down. She constantly looks out of the window throughout the scene.*

DAVID (*looking at his watch*): It is now twenty past twelve. When that boy gets home he's grounded until he's twenty-five.

ELSPETH: There's something wrong though, David. He would have phoned. He's not a bad boy.

DAVID: I know that. I worry about him too.

ELSPETH: You're never sure what to do. Are you being too strict? Are you not being strict enough? Does he know the worry we go through?

DAVID: No, he doesn't, Elspeth. He will when he has kids of his own.

ELSPETH: Wait a minute, there's somebody coming. It looks like a girl.

DAVID: If he's wearing a dress I'll disown him.

ELSPETH: It's not David, you fool.

The doorbell rings. ELSPETH *exits USL.*

DAVID *comes DSC as the lights go down to a spot*

DAVID: It's not easy being a parent. Think about it. You want your kid to do well in life. You want the best for them. You want them to be proud of you like you're proud of them. But they don't know that. They think that all you do is nag and shout at them. But you do it out of concern. You held them in your arms when they were a baby and you were there to pick them up when they fell. You wiped their tears when they cried and listened to them when they were worried. And then they hit their teens in no time at all and think they don't need you. They want to find their own way in life and start arguing with every little thing. And I know that sometimes all they want is an arm around them like they did years before. And they want to hear their daddy's voice saying 'There, there. It'll be all right.' But I can't do that. It's not how I was brought up. And I hate myself for it.

Lights come up and ELSPETH *and* JENNIFER *enter.*

ELSPETH: David, this is Jennifer. She's a friend of Jimmy's. She's got something to say.

DAVID: Do you know where my son is?

JENNIFER: I think so. He started working in that carnival just outside town. There's funny things happen there.

DAVID: What do you mean 'funny things'?

JENNIFER: I went down and... People at school talk about the man that runs the *Read Your Future* tent. There's something funny about him. Jimmy's gone away with him.

DAVID *grabs his jacket.*

DAVID: Right, lead the way. I'll batter his melt in!

They all exit.

SCENE FOUR Happy Coconut Day

CAPTAIN BLACK DOG *is shouting to his crew through the howl of a storm.*

CAPTAIN BLACK DOG: Heave to, lads! Splice the main brace!

BILLY FLOWERS: We're at the edge of the world, Captain! We're going to perish!

QUELCH: There's only death now lads!

ONE-EYED TOM: Captain, where have you taken us?

CAPTAIN BLACK DOG: Ye scurvy dogs! Hold tight! Have faith in good old Captain Black Dog!

The noise is now deafening. There are flashes of light through the darkness. Screams of terror.

Silence.

SCENE FIVE Kitty's Saloon Day

The COWBOYS *are lying around at tables and on the floor, drunk and unconscious. A flash and a bang and the* PIRATES *are flung on from USC.*

CAPTAIN BLACK DOG: What manner of devil work is this, me hearties?

BILLY FLOWERS: They smell worse than us Captain.

CAPTAIN BLACK DOG: Not possible, Billy Flowers.

ONE-EYED TOM: They be knocked out with the grog!

CAPTAIN BLACK DOG: Quietly, lads. Let's go and find some treasure.

They exit CSR.

There is a flash and a bang. UNGER *comes flying out from USC.*

UNGER: What in the name of the wee man is going on? I'm going to have to change my pants!

ANNIE MANTEE *comes to and walks up to* UNGER.

ANNIE: Come up and see me sometime.

She collapses.

UNGER: Right, Barry, pull yourself together. You're a hardman. You frighten people. It's what you do best. Now, find the old guy and get all the gen on this time travel. It could make me rich. Oh, and that's right, get scabby boy and pummel him into dust! I don't know which would give me the greatest pleasure.

He exits USR.

SCENE SIX Tent Night

DAVID, ELSPETH and JENNIFER enter from USL

TOGETHER: Hello! Anyone about!

DAVID: It's deserted.

ELSPETH: We can look about for clues.

DAVID: Aye, right, Sherlock.

DAVID picks up a cowboy hat and puts it on.

DAVID: I always wanted to be a cowboy.

He walks USC and goes behind the curtain. Lights start to flicker.

DAVID: Elspeth! Help me!

His arm is sticking out.

ELSPETH: Hold on! I'll get you!

She grabs onto his hand but is pulled through with him. She screams. Her arm is sticking through.

ELSPETH: I've got you, David! Jennifer! Pull us out!

JENNIFER grabs ELSPETH'S hand and is pulled in.

They all scream as there is a flash and a bang.

Silence.

The lights go down.

There is another flash and bang.

The ROMAN CENTURION steps out from USC.

ROMAN CENTURION: Not again. I think I'll just stay here. I've got travel sickness. And my skirt's getting rusty.

END OF ACT 2

ACT THREE
SCENE ONE Cellar Early evening

JIMMY *is up at the door USR.* MEPHIS *is sitting on a box CS whittling.* KITTY *is looking around.*

JIMMY: It's no good Mr Mephis, there's no way out. We're in here and the key's on the other side.

He stops DSC.

MEPHIS: I like whittling, Jimmy. Helps me concentrate. Helps me think things through. *(He looks over to* KITTY*)* Claustrophobia.

JIMMY: What?

MEPHIS: Nothing. So right now I've been thinking about escapologists.

JIMMY: Escapwhatigists?

MEPHIS: People whose business it is to escape from things. Now of these people there's one name that springs to mind – Harry Houdini.

JIMMY: Harry who?

MEPHIS: Dini. That's right.

KITTY: I don't like this. Enclosed spaces get me panicky.

JIMMY: It's called claustro… phobia. *(He looks at* MEPHIS.*)* How did you…?

MEPHIS: Never mind that. Houdini could escape from almost any box or prison. Chains couldn't hold him and manacles he shook off. What did get him, though, was a prison cell. But it was a very unusual story.

JIMMY: Why?

MEPHIS: Because, Jimmy, they led him to the cell and put him inside. Once he was inside they closed the door and made a big ceremony of turning the key in the lock, thus incarcerating him in a twelve by twelve cell. Houdini was a master with locks so he found a nail on the floor and proceeded to pick the lock. He had done this many times and was always free in seconds. He would listen carefully for the click… but it didn't come.

MEPHIS walks up to the door.

MEPHIS: And do you know why it didn't come, my young friend?

He turns the handle.

Because, Jimmy, it was never locked.

He slowly opens the door.

JIMMY *(excited)*: It's open! We're free!

He starts to run towards the open door.

KITTY: Just a minute. How do we know that those dirty scumbags aren't waiting outside to fill us with lead?

JIMMY comes to a halt.

MEPHIS: She's right, Jimmy. Old Annie has a reputation for being a shooter. She might want to get some practice in.

JIMMY: I don't believe this. Trapped in the past, a door to freedom, and I can't move.

They all come down slowly and sit down CS.

The lights go down to a soft glow. Music to JENNIFER creeps in softly.

KATIE and MEPHIS have their heads lowered.

What follows should have the effect of a dream sequence.

JENNIFER walks on from CSL.

JENNIFER'S SONG 2

Our soft and sad goodbyes
They're said without a care
They fall like summer rain
Another place somewhere
And deep within my heart
The memory will shine
Of how I held you close
The moment you were mine
The turn of time and tide
With you close by my side
Jennifer...

JENNIFER: Jimmy, why don't you come home?

JIMMY stands up.

JIMMY: Jennifer, I can't just now.

JENNIFER: We're all worried about you. I miss you.

JIMMY: I miss you too.

JENNIFER: Come back, Jimmy... Come back...

She disappears as the lights go down to blackout on that part of the stage.

JIMMY: Jennifer...

He comes DSC

JIMMY: It's funny. Sometimes you want to be away from everyone, but once you are you miss them. I'm always arguing with my parents. It seems like that's all we do now. I don't look tidy enough, my hair's a mess, I'm late for dinner, I'm late getting in, I'm not working hard enough at school, I'm too cheeky. If it's not one thing it's another. But I'll tell you this, right now, at this very moment, I miss them.

Lights come up CSR . DAVID and ELSPETH are talking.

DAVID: Elspeth, my heart's breaking.

ELSPETH: I know. He doesn't know how much we care.

DAVID: I know. He thinks that we're just here to shout at him. Maybe we do that too much. Maybe he hates us.

JIMMY: I don't. I don't hate you.

DAVID: If I could only hear his voice again, see him.

JIMMY: I'm here, dad. Can't you see me? Can't you hear me? I miss you so much. I miss home.

ELSPETH: Wherever he is I just hope that he's safe.

JIMMY: I'm here, mum. I'm here.

The lights fade to blackout on DAVID and ELSPETH.

JIMMY (*shouting*): I want out of here!

The PIRATES rush in screaming. They are waving swords and knives about.

KITTY (*scared*): Who are you? What do you want?

CAPTAIN BLACK DOG: Captain Black Dog and his motley crew at your service, my lovely doxy.

They all bow to KITTY.

MEPHIS: Why hello, Captain.

CAPTAIN BLACK DOG: Hooray! It's me old pal, Mr Mephis! How are you, you old land lubber ye?

MEPHIS: Captain, we have to get out of here, and quickly. If we don't then a black hole will engulf us all. We'll all be sucked into cyber-space. Baryonic dark matter will be our lot.

CAPTAIN BLACK DOG: Don't have a clue what you're on about, but it don't seem pleasant.

Enter DAVID, ELSPETH, and JENNIFER.

JIMMY *(excited)*: Mum! Dad! Jennifer! How did you get here?

DAVID: We came to take you home, son.

JENNIFER: We'll have to hurry. Those cowboys are starting to wake up.

MEPHIS: Right. Black Dog, you and your crew keep them busy while I stitch the curtain. Before the last stitch everybody pile through. We'll all be sent spinning to our own time.

CAPTAIN BLACK DOG *(shouting)*: Right, lads! Are we up for a fight?

ALL: Aye!

They all exit through door, except JIMMY and JENNIFER.

JIMMY: Jennifer, I've missed you.

JENNIFER: I missed you too.

They hug each other.

JIMMY: Let's go.

UNGER *appears at the doorway.*

UNGER: Well isn't that so romantic. Scabby boy and his scabess.

JENNIFER: You don't frighten us, Unger. There's a lot tougher than you out there.

UNGER: Tougher than me? You mean that bunch of alkies on the bar floor?

UNGER *walks towards them.*

CAPTAIN BLACK DOG *appears in the doorway behind him.*

UNGER: We've got unfinished business.

JIMMY: Keep away from us Unger. Your days are numbered. I'm sick of you and all your threats. Stuff them and stuff you!

UNGER: Big words. Is that to impress the little lady here? How about if I just kill you both? Leave you for the rats in this cellar.

CAPTAIN BLACK DOG *comes quietly up behind* UNGER *and whispers in his ear.*

CAPTAIN BLACK DOG: And how's about you come along with me and me crew and we hang your gizzards from the yard-arm?

UNGER *(taking fright)*: What the… Who are you? Look I wasn't really going to kill them. I'm only a bully.

CAPTAIN BLACK DOG: I don't rightly understand this word, lad. But I do know a snake when I hear it hiss. And little snakes become big snakes unless they be cut down. Now get your carcass out that door.

JIMMY: I owe you, Captain.

They exit.

Lights are snapped off.

SCENE TWO Saloon Night

ALL *and* COWGIRLS *are standing looking mean and nasty.*

Enter PIRATES, MEPHIS, DAVID, ELSPETH *and* KITTY, *followed by* JIMMY, CAPTAIN, UNGER *and* JENNIFER. *They all face each other, glaring.*

One at a time the PIRATES *take out their swords and daggers.*

MEPHIS *takes out his giant needle and thread.*

MEPHIS *(quietly)*: You have to keep them busy while Jimmy and I stitch up the curtain.

CAPTAIN BLACK DOG: Busy? Busy be my middle name.

MEPHIS *(to ALL)*: Ladies and gentlemen, we are gathered here for a purpose. Some of us are a trifle out of joint. We wish to depart and return to our homes. But I cannot leave without first repairing that curtain.

ANNIE: What? That li'l ol' curtain back there? Shucks, that ain't nothing to be botherin' your old grey head about. But if you're up for deeeepart, then don't let us stand in your way.

MEPHIS: Now Annie, you know as well as me that some of your boys have been poking their noses where they shouldn't be. They've been troubling time itself, and that can't go on.

ANNIE: The gang have just been havin' a bit of fun. Now surely you and your friends wouldn't begrudge them that?

MEPHIS: Fun's fun, but this goes way beyond the rules of the world. You know this, Annie.

CAPTAIN BLACK DOG: If you'd just like to sit down and let Mr Mephis do his work then we can be off without any bloodshed.

ANNIE: That just can't happen. We run this place now. And we control that curtain.

MEPHIS: There's nothing more to be said then. Ladies and gentlemen, let the fight begin.

Shouts from everyone. A fight ensues. During the fight MEPHIS and JIMMY stitch the curtain USC and everyone apart from the COWBOYS and COWGIRLS escape through it by the end.

Once the last characters are through the lights come up.

MEPHIS *(voice offstage)*: Two more stitches, Jimmy! Wait a minute, who's this?

Through the curtain the ROMAN CENTURION and MRS CULPEPPER enter. The ROMAN CENTURION has a parchment in his hand.

ROMAN CENTURION: I rescued this Vestal earlier. I got lost again.

UNGER enters from CSR. He has been hiding while the fighting has been going on.

UNGER: Old man, get me out of this freak show or else.

MEPHIS: You're hardly in a position to issue threats, Mr Unger.

UNGER grabs MEPHIS by the neck and starts choking him.

The ROMAN CENTURION *opens up the parchment and reads:*

ROMAN CENTURION: Unger. Barry. Twenty first century. School bully. Cheat. Coward.

UNGER loosens his grip.

ROMAN CENTURION: Small time crook. Graduates to armed robbery with violence.

UNGER *(proudly)*: I knew I'd make it big time.

ROMAN CENTURION: Murderer. Murders... James... I can't read the next bit. This is an old document.

UNGER: One little murder.

ROMAN CENTURION: You kill the keeper of Time. Chaos has come. The end.

The ROMAN CENTURION *grabs* UNGER.

ROMAN CENTURION: I've come to sweep up.

They all step back through the curtain.

Lights down to blackout.

Silence.

SCENE THREE Tent Night

DAVID, ELSPETH, JENNIFER, JIMMY, MEPHIS, CAPTAIN BLACK DOG, MRS CULPEPPER, UNGER, ROMAN CENTURION, KITTY, *all come tumbling out from the curtain USC.*

JIMMY: Home!

JENNIFER: At last!

ELSPETH: It's way past our bedtime!

DAVID: We'll make sure you get home first, Jennifer.

JENNIFER: Thanks. I don't know what my parents will say about me being away.

MEPHIS: Don't you worry about that. No time has passed. We have returned just before we left.

DAVID: I think I want to wake up tomorrow and find this was all a dream.

ELSPETH: Why don't you come around for tea next week?

JENNIFER: That would be great.

CAPTAIN BLACK DOG: I prefer rum, missus!

ELSPETH: Oh, of course, the invite goes out to you all.

DAVID: If you think I'm letting that midden into my house...

CAPTAIN BLACK DOG: What be a midden, me hearties?

MEPHIS: It's a vessel for rubbish, Captain.

CAPTAIN BLACK DOG: I've captained a few of those right enough. Talking of which, Mr Mephis, where be me crew?

MEPHIS: I dropped them off on the way here.

CAPTAIN BLACK DOG: Now wasn't that clever of ye?

MEPHIS: Captain, you and the centurion will have to go back. Each to your own place. Unger, you will be an evil and dangerous man when you grow up. You will cause untold damage to the universe.

UNGER: Cheers, mate.

MEPHIS: You don't belong here. And, Jimmy, neither do I.

JIMMY: What do you mean?

MEPHIS picks up the crystal ball and hands it to JIMMY.

MEPHIS: I want you to look after the tent, Jimmy. All the answers will be in this crystal ball. I'm tired. I've waited a thousand years for you to arrive. It's the one thing I could not do. Leave this responsibility to just anyone.

And now you're here *(with great care, he hands JIMMY the needle and thread)* and have this, my work is done. Goodbye, my friend.

MEPHIS shakes JIMMY'S hand.

JIMMY: Goodbye, Mr Mephis.

MEPHIS: And remember to switch out the tent lights. You really don't want the generator running down. Come, my friends.

ROMAN CENTURION places his hand on UNGER'S shoulder.

ROMAN CENTURION: You will come with me. There are some lions I want you to meet.

UNGER *(suddenly excited)*: A trip to the zoo! Great!

ROMAN CENTURION *(to MEPHIS)*: What's a zoo?

MEPHIS, ROMAN CENTURION, UNGER and CAPTAIN BLACK DOG exit through curtain.

ALL say goodbye.

DAVID: I'll drive everyone home. I think we've had enough excitement for today. Jimmy?

JIMMY: Sure, dad. But give me a minute with Jennifer.

Everyone exits except JENNIFER and JIMMY.

JIMMY: Jennifer, do you want to go out with me properly?

JENNIFER: Of course I do. Listen, I'd better get home. Hurry up and turn off the lights. I'll wait at the car.

She exits.

JIMMY: Mr Mephis, I think I've been waiting a thousand years for this job.

MEPHIS *(voice offstage)*: You have, Jimmy. You have.

JIMMY: Goodnight.

He switches off the lights until there is blackout.

MEPHIS *(voice offstage)*: Goodnight, Jimmy. And remember, you are the Keeper of Time. Guard it well. Our fate is in your hands.

END OF PLAY

ACTIVITIES

Plot

1 On your own or in a group, list the main incidents and important revelations in the play.

2 Write a paragraph of no more than ten sentences that describes the story.

Structure

In a play, there are several different sections, which usually happen in the order shown below:

Exposition
Where the situation and characters are introduced.

Turning point
Where the main character realises something or an event occurs that changes the course of events.

Climax
When the action and emotions reach the most exciting, dramatic point.

Resolution
Events and emotions are worked out in the aftermath of the climax and it is clear where things now stand.

1 On your own or in a group, think about the exposition, turning point, climax and resolution of *A Stitch in Time*. Write two or three sentences which explain what happens in each of these sections.

2 Read the turning point again (Act III, Scene One). Write an analysis which shows how the writer creates impact in the turning point. You should analyse:

- monologue, dialogue and song

- actions of characters

- structure (in particular, the ordering of incidents close to each other to make certain points)

- atmosphere created by technical effects.

If you make a statement about the writer's technique, make sure you back it up with evidence from the play. You could try to justify the statements below and make some of your own.

- Music, lighting and dialogue combine to create an atmosphere of regret and longing for home. (Analyse the dream sequence with Jennifer.)

- At the turning point, Jimmy begins to understand his parents' feelings for him. (Analyse the position of Jimmy's monologue and the effect of his parents being unable to hear him.)

- The position of the turning point gives it greater impact. (Analyse incidents immediately before and after it.)

Writing Activities

A Stitch in Time explores several themes. The main ones are:

- bullying
- family relationships
- responsibility.

1 Think about these issues and explain in writing, or during a group discussion, what the protagonist, Jimmy, learns as a result of his experience as a time traveller.

2 Write an essay in which you explore your ideas on one of these themes.

Make sure you:

- stick to a line of thought throughout, for example:

   bullying
   bullies need to confront the consequences of their behaviour for themselves and other people

   family relationships
   family members have to communicate with each other to avoid conflict

   responsibility
   we have to accept our responsibilies in order to grow up

- introduce your line of thought in the opening paragraph

- back up your statements with examples (statistics, anecdotes of your own or from other people, logical argument)

- group connected information in paragraphs
- include a topic sentence in each paragraph (a sentence which summarises the point of the paragraph)
- link paragraphs sensibly
- come to a conclusion that summarises the statements you have made.

Dramascript Activities

Below are some tasks that let you use your own imagination and practise your own script writing. Your dialogue and stage directions should be written in the same style and layout as is used in *A Stitch in Time*.

Remember – stage directions are sections of description designed to give directors and actors information about the look and atmosphere of a production. They are separate from the words spoken by the characters – dialogue and soliloquy.

Act I, Scene One

1 Using what you read in Act I, Scene One, write stage directions describing the visual appearance of Mr Mephis and Jimmy. These should cover their costume, physical features and the way they move.

Your descriptions should help the audience understand the kind of people these characters are.

2 If you enjoy drawing, sketch the characters and add notes where necessary to explain features of their appearance.

Act I, Scene One

1 Describe the entrance of the pirates at the end of this scene through a series of tableaux. These are 'frozen' images of moments of action. Look at the entrance of the cowboys in Act I, Scene Four to see how to do this.

Think about:

- lighting
- gesture
- facial expression.

2 If your class is used to dramatic performance, act out these tableaux.

Act I, Scene Three

Re-read Act I, Scene Three. Write an alternative outcome where Jimmy stands up to Unger. Write in script style and format as shown in *A Stitch in Time*.

Act III, Scene Two

1 Describe the fight scene that takes place as Mephis and Jimmy stitch the curtain. Think about using the following techniques:

- tableaux
- slow motion
- lighting
- special effects.

Make sure you show:

- Mephis and Jimmy stitching the curtain USC
- everyone apart from the cowboys and cowgirls escaping through it at the end.

2 If your class is used to dramatic performance, act out the scene.

Further Writing Activities

1 Mr Mephis' poster declares:

You change the past, you change the future?

Think about the past – your own experiences, those of others, and events in history. What would you change? What impact would that have on the present, and even the future?

Write in any way you choose about changing the past.

2 Read the scenes including Jimmy's dad again. Imagine you are Jimmy's dad before the happy ending. Write a letter to a problem page pouring out your anxieties about your son and ask for advice on what to do about him. You should create a sense of Jimmy's dad's character based on what you know of him from the play. (You may need to read some problem pages to see the style they are written in.)

Write the reply to Jimmy's dad from the agony aunt.

3 Imagine you are Jimmy and several months have passed since you took over as the Keeper of Time from Mr Mephis. Write a letter to him letting him know how things are going. You could write about:

- what has changed in your relationships (with your parents and Jennifer)

- what difference Unger's disappearance has made

- interesting events and time travellers you have met

- what you have learned from your experience with Mr Mephis

- even the state of the curtain and your thoughts on time travel!

You should create a sense of Jimmy's character based on what you know of him from the play.

Use of Song Activities

We are sometimes given information about characters through songs.

1 Re-read the songs (the Pirates' song, the Cowboys' song, Jennifer's songs).

2 Choose one and describe what the song contributes to your understanding of the character's background, emotions, personality and so on.

3 Explain what the songs add to the action and atmosphere of the play.

4 Write the lyrics of a song by Mephis called *A Stitch in Time*. The song should express his feelings as he hands over the responsibility for stitching time to Jimmy. Think about how you might feel as an older person facing up to the fact that you are not as able as you once were to carry out your responsibilities.

If you are confident about describing music, suggest how the song should sound. Describe:

- pace
- instruments
- mood
- rhythm.

Gangsters

by

Roy McGregor

SCENE ONE Evening Bar

MAN 1 *sits at a table drinking and reading his paper. He is a bit agitated, keeps looking towards the door, obviously waiting for someone.*

BARMAID *walks over to collect the empties.*

BARMAID: You been stood up, pal?

MAN 1 *(surprised)*: What?

BARMAID: Looks like you've been stood up.

MAN 1: I'm waiting on someone.

BARMAID: I know that feeling. My husband went out for a pint of milk three years ago. I'm still waiting on him coming back.

MAN 1: I got here early.

BARMAID: Catch the worm, eh?

MAN 1: What?

BARMAID: The worm? The early bird?

MAN 1: Could you leave me in peace to finish my drink?

BARMAID: Just being friendly.

MAN 2 *enters. He is carrying a box.*

MAN 1: I'm sure you are.

BARMAID *walks away with the empties.*

MAN 1 *sees* MAN 2 *looking around and waves to him.*

MAN 2 *sees him and walks over.*

MAN 1: I see you got it.

MAN 2 *(looking at the box)*: Aye.

MAN 1: Sit down.

MAN 2 *sits down and puts the box on the table between them.*

MAN 2: It's all right. I don't want a drink.

MAN 1: I didn't ask you.

MAN 2: I know.

Pause.

Well, do you want it?

MAN 1 *(looking at the box)***:** It looks good. Were there any problems?

MAN 2: Problems? What sort of problems?

MAN 1: You know, the usual.

MAN 2: The usual? What do you mean by that? Do you think I do this all the time?

MAN 1: Sorry. I didn't mean to offend you.

BARMAID *walks over to the table.*

BARMAID: Are you getting a drink?

MAN 2: What's it got to do with you?

BARMAID: We don't like people sitting in the pub without a drink. Gives punters the wrong impression.

MAN 2 *stands up, threatening.*

MAN 2: I'll make an impression on you.

MAN 1 *puts his hand on his arm to calm him down.*

MAN 1: Sit down. We don't need trouble. Particularly tonight.

BARMAID: You heard your pal. Cool it.

BARMAID *walks away.*

MAN 2 *sits.*

Pause.

MAN 2: I came to deliver the goods. That's it. You owe me.

MAN 1 *(sighing)***:** Aye.

MAN 1 *picks up his glass. Drinks slowly.*

Lights go down to blackout.

SCENE TWO Office Night

Music plays softly in the background.

Lights come up.

A group of gangsters sit around a table. DON *is at the top of the table talking to them. To his right is* MOLL.

DON: You wonder why I have gathered you all here at this hour of the night. This is obviously a serious matter.

JUNE: Don, you know when you call we'll be there.

The group mutter their agreement.

DON: Good to hear it. I expect no less. I have, though, very bad news. It has struck me deeply.

With a pained expression he touches his heart.

VITO: You're not dying, are you, boss?

SONNY: Don't leave us.

They all start crying.

DON *(angry)*: Shut up!

They all stop immediately.

I'm not dying.

VITO: This is great news. We'll have to have a party.

MOLL: A party! Yeah!

A burst of lively music and the group stand up and start dancing. DON *is fuming.*

AL: I'll have to buy new clothes. I haven't a thing to wear. Where can I get a good suit?

FRANK: *Kenny's Klobber's* cheap. Just don't let anyone see you go in. Remember, you have a reputation to keep up.

DON *(shouting)*: Will you two shut up?

The music is cut off immediately.

There aren't going to be any parties around here.

MOLL: Yeah, cancel the party!

They all say, 'Cancel the party', 'The party is off' etc.

DON looks at them menacingly.

They all sit.

Silence.

DON: There will be no parties because there has been a robbery.

ZOOT: A robbery? But we can't get robbed. We're gangsters. We do the robbing.

DON: I never thought that I'd see the day, but that day is here, my fellow criminals.

FRANK: What did they steal, boss? It wasn't…?

A sharp intake of breath and a look of shock from everyone.

DON: Yes, it was. It was in a box in my safe and some low down dirty rat walked in and took it from under my very nose.

ZOOT: Kill him!

FRANK: Pulverise him!

SONNY: Rip out his liver and feed it to the cat!

VITO: Tear off his head!

ZOOT: He'll be swimming with da fishes!

FRANK: A concrete overcoat!

DON: Silence, you mugs!

Silence.

We have to find out who it was first.

DON opens up a folder on his desk.

DON: I have here a list of names. Each of them is in an envelope. You will pair off. You will question whoever is named in your envelope. After you have questioned them you will introduce them to the big sleep. You got that?

They all nod in agreement.

DON *nods to* MOLL. *She stands up holding the envelopes out.*

MOLL: Okay, Zoot and Frank step forward and take an envelope.

ZOOT *and* FRANK *step forward and take an envelope.*

ZOOT and FRANK *(together)*: You have spoken, so let it be done, Don.

DON *nods.* ZOOT *and* FRANK *sit.*

MOLL: Vito and Sonny step forward.

VITO *and* SONNY *step forward.*

Take one envelope, boys.

VITO *takes one envelope.*

VITO and SONNY *(together)*: You have spoken, so let it be done, Don.

DON *nods.* VITO *and* SONNY *sit.*

MOLL: April and June step forward. Come on girls, we don't have all night.

APRIL *and* JUNE *step forward.*

You know the routine. Take an envelope.

JUNE *takes an envelope.*

APRIL and JUNE *(together)*: You have spoken, so it's gonna be done, Don. Whatever.

DON *raises his eyes to the ceiling. He is annoyed.*

The girls sit down.

MOLL: Okay, Al and Tony step forward.

They step forward.

Take the last envelope.

AL *takes the envelope.*

AL and TONY *(together)*: You have spoken, so let it be done, Don.

DON *nods. They all sit.*

DON: Everybody open your envelopes.

They all tear open their envelopes.

Okay. You have in your mitts the name of the persons who must be questioned. I wish you well.

DON *and* MOLL *stand and walk to door USR.*

I am tired and I am going to bed. You too must have a good sleep, for tomorrow the work begins. One thing is certain, when I find out who has committed this most awful of deeds I will plunge them into an eternity of darkness.

He claps his hands and the lights are snapped off. Darkness.

Like that.

SCENE THREE Street Morning

Creepy music plays.

DANGEROUS DAVE *is walking down the street. He is being followed by* APRIL *and* JUNE. *He keeps stopping and looking behind him but they keep diving into the doorways.*

Eventually JUNE *runs up to him.*

JUNE *(breathless)*: Excuse me, could you help? I think I'm being followed.

DANGEROUS DAVE: That's funny, so am I.

APRIL *creeps up behind him and hits him with a blunt instrument. He collapses to the ground.*

APRIL: Right, you bring the car around. I'll watch him.

JUNE: Right.

JUNE *runs off.*

APRIL *(to audience)*: It's not easy being a gangster, y'know. When I was young I really wanted to work in a bank. Now I just rob them. If you're going to do something in life then make sure you do it well. I'm the best criminal in town.

Sound of a car approaching.

Here's the car now.

She starts to pick up DANGEROUS DAVE.

Come on you. Dangerous Dave? Let me tell you, sunshine, you don't know dangerous.

Lights fade to blackout.

SCENE FOUR Restaurant Day

VITO *and* SONNY *sit at a restaurant table looking at menus.* SONNY *is looking out from above and from the side of his menu, his eyes searching.*

VITO: This is my favourite kind of food. I think I'll have the ravioli.

SONNY: What are you talking about?

VITO: On the menu. The ravioli sounds good. Although the spaghetti would be quite nice. Washed down with a small Chianti.

SONNY: Spaghetti? Ravioli? Chianti? You're not here to fill your face. You're here to do a job. The boss wants Fingers Correlo questioned. This is where the slimeball works.

VITO: I know, but since we were here I thought that we might have a bite to eat.

SONNY: Don't mix business with pleasure. First we question Fingers, then you eat.

VITO: I don't know, I'm not at my best when I'm hungry. I'm liable to lose my head and...

He pulls a gun from his jacket pocket and starts to wave it around.

blow his head clean off his shoulders!

SONNY *(panicking)*: Put that away. Do you want to get us pinched for carrying illegal weapons?

VITO: Sorry, Sonny.

He puts his gun away.

SONNY: Right, there he is over there. Chatting up the girls as usual. Attract his attention.

VITO *stands up and starts shouting and waving his arms about wildly.*

VITO: Waiter! Waiter! Yoo-hoo!

SONNY *(pulling him down)*: Sit down, you fool.

VITO *(sitting)*: Sorry, Sonny.

SONNY: Remind me not to take you out to dinner.

The waiter comes over. It is FINGERS CORRELO. VITO *and* SONNY *are hiding behind their menus.*

FINGERS: Ciao, baby. What can I get you hungry gentlemen today?

SONNY *(laying down his menu)*: Hello, Fingers. Or should I call you Romeo?

FINGERS *(shocked)*: Sonny!

VITO *(laying down his menu)*: Would you recommend the garlic or plain ciabatta?

SONNY: Our boss is not a happy man, Fingers. We want you to cheer him up in these desperate times.

FINGERS *(nervous)*: Of course, if I could... but... I'm working, you see.

SONNY: Get your coat. You're coming with us.

FINGERS: No… I can't.

In a flash VITO *has removed his gun and pulled* FINGERS *down onto the table. The gun is at his head.*

VITO: As my much admired associate says, you're coming with us. If you hesitate once more I will blow your head off your shoulders.

SONNY *(to audience)*: Vito may not be subtle, but he cuts to the chase. *(To* FINGERS*)* Fingers – or should I say Romeo? Get your coat.

FINGERS: Of course I'll get my coat.

VITO *lets him go.*

Let's get this sorted. I have nothing to hide.

SONNY *and* VITO *stand.*

VITO: Before we go, Fingers, one question.

FINGERS *(scared)*: Anything. I am an honest man.

VITO: Very good. Ciabatta: garlic or plain?

SONNY *and* VITO *put their arms around* FINGERS' *shoulders and walk him out. The lights go down as music plays.*

SCENE FIVE Street Day

MAD DOG MCLINTOCK *is up a ladder cleaning windows.*

Two people are standing at opposite ends of the stage with a newspaper in front of them They drop the newspapers. They are FRANK *and* ZOOT. *They walk to the bottom of the ladder.*

ZOOT: You missed a bit there.

MAD DOG: Don't tell me how to clean windows, ya numpty! I can clean windows!

FRANK *shakes the ladder.*

FRANK: That ladder's none too safe, my friend.

MAD DOG: Heh! Watch it!

ZOOT *takes off his glasses.*

ZOOT: Think you can clean my lenses?

MAD DOG: I'll come down there and thump you!

FRANK: No need to be aggressive. We're just making polite conversation.

ZOOT: Mad Dog, come down. We want a word with you.

MAD DOG: You can call me Mr McLintock.

ZOOT: Mr McLintock could we possibly have a word?

MAD DOG: What about?

ZOOT: About a robbery.

MAD DOG *(suddenly nervous)*: I don't know anything about a robbery. I want to live a decent life. I've given up my criminal past. Leave me alone.

ZOOT *(to* FRANK*)*: Suddenly he's not a tough guy. *(To* MAD DOG*)* We can't continue shouting in the street. Come down and we'll discuss it like gentlemen.

MAD DOG: I'm not coming down unless I get a promise that there'll be no violence perpetrated on my person.

FRANK *(to* ZOOT*)*: What does that mean?

ZOOT: He doesn't want us to beat him up.

FRANK: Look at the size of him. He must know who we are. Can we shoot him?

ZOOT: Not until we question him.

FRANK *(to* MAD DOG*)*: You can trust us.

MAD DOG: Okay, I'll come down.

He starts to come down. FRANK *and* ZOOT *pull him down the last few rungs and throw him against the wall.*

FRANK: How about if we tear out your eyes?

ZOOT: Rip out your throat?

FRANK: Punch out your lights?

ZOOT: Kick in your face?

FRANK: Stab you?

ZOOT: Chib you?

FRANK: Slash you?

ZOOT: Pull out your lungs?

FRANK: Cut off your legs?

ZOOT: Chop up your liver?

MAD DOG: I'm getting the impression that you guys aren't too happy.

FRANK: What makes you say that?

ZOOT: You're coming with us to answer a few questions.

> MAD DOG *looks slowly at* ZOOT *and* FRANK.

MAD DOG: Can I take my bladder and ucket? I mean ludder and backet. I mean...

> *Lights go down to blackout.*

SCENE SIX Dark Room Night

> *A spotlight falls on a table. A box – the same one from scene one – sits on the table.*

Voice Offstage (*quietly*): Well. Here we are. What a fuss. What a fuss over something as small and innocent as me.

> *Pause.*

I should be used to it by now. Oh, the trouble that I've caused over the years. Oh, dear me, the trouble. Murders and tortures. It really is shocking. This is going back a thousand years. And the funny thing is that very few have seen me, and those that have... well, what bad luck has fallen upon them. And they still come for me. Oh, the butchery... the mayhem... the death...

Sound of a door slamming.

Lights come up.

MAN 1 *from Scene One enters.*

MAN 1: At last I can find out what's in this box. They say that you're cursed. Ha! I don't believe any of that nonsense.

He stands at the table ready to open the box. His hands go closer to it. The doorbell rings.

What? Who is that? I'm not expecting anyone.

The doorbell rings.

Just a minute!

He throws a cloth over the box. The doorbell rings more urgently.

All right! All right! Just coming!

The doorbell rings. He exits.

MAN 1 (*voice offstage*): Oh, it's you. What is it? Come in before you're seen.

MAN 2 *enters followed by* MAN 1.

MAN 2: I need the box back. There's been a mistake.

MAN 1: A mistake? There can't be a mistake. You can't have it back. I've got a buyer.

MAN 2: You really don't understand. I'm not asking you.

He pulls out a gun.

I'm telling you.

MAN 1: It's not here. I got rid of it.

MAN 2 *slowly pulls the cloth from the table, exposing the box.*

MAN 2 *smiles.*

MAN 2: You were saying?

MAN 1 *(frightened)*: Look, let's talk about this… Please… I made a mistake… Of course you can have it back… Don't kill me… Please…

MAN 2 *shoots MAN 1 who falls to the floor.*

MAN 2 *takes the box and exits.*

Blackout.

SCENE SEVEN Office Night

Music plays softly in the background. The gang sit around the table. MOLL is not present. DON stands at the head of the table. He has folders in front of him.

DON: Well, here we are. Back where we started.

He picks up the folders.

I have your reports here. And they are very detailed and accurate, and… dare I say – gruesome.

ZOOT *(smiling)*: Thanks, boss.

DON: What I don't have is the item that was stolen from me. This makes me very angry.

ZOOT: We did the best we could, boss.

DON: Your best obviously isn't good enough. By the way, where's Moll?

JUNE: She said that she had to powder her nose.

DON: She's been gone half an hour. How big's her nose? April and June, go and find her.

APRIL and JUNE *(together)*: Okay, Don.

> *They exit.*

DON: Where was I? Ah, yes. You're all about as useful as a bicycle for a fish.

ZOOT *(smiling)*: Or a chocolate teapot, boss.

DON: Come here, Zoot.

> ZOOT *goes over to* DON.

> DON *slaps his face.*

Don't be cheeky. Now sit down.

ZOOT: Sorry, boss.

> *He sits down.*

DON: I'll tell all of you now, and it breaks my heart to say it, but I think that this was an inside job.

> *Shocked, they all look at each other.*

SCENE EIGHT Garden Night

It is a warm evening. The moon is full in the sky. MOLL *paces up and down anxiously. After a few moments* MAN 2 *arrives carrying the box.*

MAN 2: Moll?

MOLL: You're here. At last. You got it?

MAN 2: What do you think this is? A box of chocolates?

MOLL: Give me it.

MAN 2: Just a minute. There's the little question of ten thousand pounds that you owe me.

MOLL: What do you mean? I don't owe you. You were supposed to fence the goods. Now I want them back there's really nothing for you to do.

MAN 2: There was the little matter of a murder that I committed for you. You owe me big time. And if I'm not paid then maybe your boyfriend will find out what a little cheating two-timer you are.

MOLL: Don't threaten me.

MAN 2: You're hardly in a position to make threats. Unless of course you intend killing me.

MOLL: Maybe that's not such a bad idea. I'll tell you what. You leave the box on the ground here and nobody will find out anything about you. You can be a free man.

MAN 2: But Moll, I'm already a free man. I can march right in there and tell Don everything. I'm sure he'd probably reward me for all my help. And for opening his eyes to you. You see, Moll, I am a free man.

MOLL *takes a gun from her pocket.*

MOLL: No, my friend, you are a dead man.

She shoots him. He falls down dead.

APRIL *and* JUNE *enter.*

APRIL: Moll, what have you done?

JUNE: You've killed him, in cold blood. We watched you.

MOLL: He asked for it. He was trying to blackmail me.

APRIL: What about?

MOLL: I had dinner with Fingers Correlo.

JUNE: You what? If Don finds out he'll rag doll you.

MOLL: I know. That's why you've got to help me.

She picks up the box.

APRIL: Is that Don's box?

MOLL: That piece of scum that I just shot stole it. I was tipped off that he'd be willing to sell it to me. I arranged this meeting and then he said the money wasn't enough. Greed. All I wanted to do was return the box to the man I love, Don.

JUNE: Moll, we're your friends. We'll help you.

MOLL: I knew I could rely on you.

She hands the box to APRIL.

Sneak this back into Don's safe.

APRIL: What good will that do?

MOLL: He'll be happy if the box is returned.

APRIL: And what if he catches us?

MOLL: It's all right. All he's concerned about is the return of that stupid box.

JUNE: Okay, we'll do it.

MOLL: Right. I'll get rid of this body. See ya later, girls.

MOLL *lugs off the body.*

Lights down slowly into blackout.

SCENE NINE Office Night

As end of Scene Seven.

DON: Sometimes, boys, things get a little lax. Not much happens and everybody gets a little sloppy. They begin to question what they're doing. This is bad. Sometimes this will lead to thoughts of another nature. These thoughts might lead them to question who is the boss. This is very bad.

Pause.

There have been dark deeds happening in the last few days, you are aware of this. In the midst of this darkness you have proven yourselves loyal, and that will be rewarded. Some, though, have not been as respectful as they could have, and examples have to be made. For this I am sorry. But such is life. I cannot walk in the dark. Boys, open some champagne. Tonight we must celebrate.

He exits.

FRANK: What was that all about?

ZOOT: Beats me.

SONNY: Sometimes the boss frightens me.

MOLL *arrives from the garden.*

MOLL: What's that about the boss?

SONNY: I said sometimes he frightens me.

MOLL'S *eyes widen with fear.*

MOLL: Where is he?

VITO: He said that he had to make examples.

MOLL *(frightened)*: Oh no!

She runs out.

SONNY: Come on boys! Champagne!

Blackout.

SCENE TEN Don's Room Night

In the corner, lit by a soft spotlight, is a safe. The rest is in darkness. APRIL *and* JUNE *enter. They are whispering.*

APRIL: I can't see a thing.

JUNE: Over there. In the corner. The safe.

They come into the light.

JUNE: You keep a lookout. I'll crack the combination.

JUNE *gets down and starts to turn the dial on the safe.*

The lights are snapped on and DON *is standing in the corner.*

JUNE *and* APRIL *looked shocked.*

DON: You broke my heart, girls. Now let me break yours.

DON *shoots* APRIL. *She falls down dead,*

JUNE: I beg you, Don. You don't understand… It was…

DON *shoots* JUNE.

DON: I understand only too well, June.

JUNE: This is a mistake…

She dies.

MOLL *enters.*

MOLL *(shocked)*: Don, what…

DON: They betrayed me, Moll.

He stares at her. She crumbles under the stare.

MOLL: They didn't. It was me. I betrayed you. I had dinner with Fingers the night of the burglary. We got drunk and thought it would be a laugh to steal something from you. Once I saw what Fingers took, I thought I could make some money so I got someone to sell it. I quickly realised my mistake and tried to put things back to normal. It was all my fault, Don.

DON: Don't you think I know that, Moll?

MOLL: You know?

DON: Fingers came to me and confessed everything. Very noble of the lad. A little late, I thought, so I slit his throat. As for April and June. They've been getting a bit too lippy of late. When they tried to collude with you that was the last straw. They really had to die.

MOLL: And now you're going to kill me?

DON: Of course not, sweet Moll. You've learned a hard lesson. Come and let's celebrate that Moll has seen the error of her ways. She has returned to me a new woman. Let's have some champagne.

They exit.

DON *turns out the light.*

Spot still on safe. The box is on top.

VOICE OFFSTAGE: Well, that was a surprise. More deaths, though. That's never a surprise. Of course Don won't keep me. Greed gets the better of everyone. As a matter of fact here's someone now. I'd better keep quiet.

In the dark a FIGURE *enters and slowly picks up the box. The figure exits.*

Fade to blackout.

END OF PLAY

ACTIVITIES

Plot

Sequencing

Here is a list of incidents that happen in *Gangsters*. Write them out in the order in which they happen in the play. You might find it easier to cut out each statement and rearrange them on your desk. Your teacher may ask you and another pupil to work together on this.

✂

MAD DOG is taken away for questioning by ZOOT and FRANK.

DON is informed that MOLL is powdering her nose.

MAN 2 and the BARMAID have an argument.

MOLL hands out envelopes to the gang.

MAN 1 is shot down dead.

VITO and SONNY pick up FINGERS.

DON kills APRIL and JUNE.

Plot summary

A plot summary is a short explanation of what happens in a play or story.

Once you have finished reading *Gangsters*, write a plot summary of the play. You will need a copy of the play at hand to refer to. It may help to make a list of the **main** incidents before you start. You should not use any dialogue from the play, tell the story in your own words.

Structure

In a play there are several different sections, which usually happen in the order shown below:

Exposition

At the beginning of a play, the situation and characters are introduced. It is where we find out what is happening and who it is happening to.

Turning point

Where the main character realises something, or something unexpected happens that changes the course of events.

Climax

Near the very end of a play, where it is at its most exciting and dramatic point. All plays build to this point.

Resolution

Events and emotions are resolved after the climax, and it is now clear where things stand.

1 On your own or in a group, think about the exposition, turning point, climax and resolution of *Gangsters*. Write two or three sentences which explain what happens in each of these sections.

2 Read the climax again (Scene Ten). Write a paragraph or two which explain how the climax is made exciting by the writer. You should analyse:

- dialogue
- actions of characters
- atmosphere created by technical effects.

If you make a statement about the writer's technique, make sure you back it up with evidence from the play. Look at the example below to help you.

Statement Contrast in atmosphere is used to heighten the impact of the climax.

Evidence The scene immediately before the climax ends with a celebration when SONNY calls out 'Champagne!' This contrasts with the frightened whispering of APRIL and JUNE immediately afterwards, and makes their murder seem even more shocking.

Motivation and character

Motivation is the reason characters take the actions that they do. The questions below ask you to think about the behaviour and motivation of the characters in *Gangsters*.

DON

1 At what point do you think that DON might have suspected the loyalty of APRIL and JUNE?

2 How does DON find out about MOLL's involvement with the theft?

3 Why does he let MOLL live?

VITO and SONNY

1 Who is the most professional of these two characters? How do we know?

2 How do we know that VITO is a dangerous man?

3 Why do you think these characters follow DON's orders?

APRIL and JUNE

1 Is there any reason not to believe APRIL when she says that she's the best criminal in town?

2 Why do you think that APRIL and JUNE try to help MOLL?

3 Do these characters deserve to die?

Writing

Dramascript

Imagine that between Scenes Six and Seven Don's henchmen and henchwomen interrogate their suspects. There could be three extra scenes focusing on DANGEROUS DAVE, MAD DOG and FINGERS.

Write one or more of these extra scenes. What you write should provoke a reaction from your audience – before you write, decide if you want them to scream with laughter or fear.

You should:

- write in the style of the *Gangsters* script
- lay out your script like *Gangsters*
- use dialogue and stage directions
- use information you have about the characters from the play, the character cards for the suspects, and your own imagination

- make sure your scene(s) make sense with what happens later in the play.

If your class is used to performing scripts, act out one or more of these scenes.

Short story

Write a short story entitled 'The Box' which explains the mystery of the box in *Gangsters*. It should be narrated in the first person (this means that the box is telling its own story), and it should begin and end with the lines below.

Opening   You'd think I'd be tired of it after all these years, but watching them fall for the same thing time after time still amuses me very much.

Ending   Well there you have it. The same old story, I'm afraid. It seems that greed still gets the better of everyone…

The Bone Orchard

by

Roy McGregor

CHARACTERS

ALICIA
ANNE
BERNADETTE
KIMBERLEY
SHAZ
THOMAS
ALI
DANIEL
DAVID
GHOULS

SCENE ONE Graveyard Night

Darkness. Music plays. Lights come up to give the effect of a moonlit night.

Screams. ALICIA *enters from CSL. She is running and screaming. She crosses to CSR and exits.*

Silence.

A lot of screams. A group of GHOULS *enter CSL and run across to CS. They stop and look at the audience. They look to each other and then run off CSR.*

Silence.

Music plays. ALICIA *enters from USC. She is walking in backwards, slowly, afraid. At the same time* BERNADETTE *enters from CSR. Again she is walking backwards towards CS. At the same time* SHAZ *enters from CSL. She is also terrified walking backwards towards CS. At the same point they all meet CS.*

The music stops and they all scream.

ALICIA *(panicking)*: Bernadette! Shaz! You're alive? I thought they'd got you.

SHAZ: No thanks to you.

BERNADETTE: This is all your fault, Alicia. You'd better get us out of this.

ALICIA: This isn't happening, is it? It doesn't seem real. Where am I?

ANNE *(voice offstage)*: Alicia!

The lights start to go down.

BERNADETTE: Help us, Alicia. Help us.

ALICIA: I can't. I can't help myself.

ANNE *(voice offstage)*: Alicia, I won't tell you again! You'll be late!

GHOULS *come out from behind the curtains. They move slowly towards CS.* BERNADETTE *and* SHAZ *sink to their knees, frightened.* ALICIA *moves DSC. She turns her back to the audience. The music comes up loudly, followed by the sound of loud screaming.*

The GHOULS *surround* BERNADETTE *and* SHAZ *threateningly.*

ALICIA *(screaming)*: Stop this! This is not happening! I will not have this!

The lights are snapped off as is the sound.

SCENE TWO Bedroom Morning

In the dark ALICIA *screams. Lights come up, bright. We find her sitting up in bed terrified.* ANNE *stands beside her holding a cup of tea. On the bedside table are some books and jotters.*

ANNE: Alicia, you're having a dream. What goes on in your head?

ALICIA: You don't want to know, mum.

ANNE: Here, have some tea and get up.

ALICIA *takes the cup of tea and drinks.*

ALICIA: Cheers.

ANNE: Thirsty girl.

She picks up a jotter from the table.

No wonder you can't get a proper night's sleep. Homework's for after school, not before you go to sleep.

ALICIA: I know, mum. I just couldn't finish it.

ANNE: What is it? English? I'll help you downstairs.

ALICIA: What's an anagram?

ANNE: When you mix up the letters of a word to form another word.

ALICIA: What's the point in that?

The sound of a cordless telephone. ANNE *takes a phone from her pocket. She answers it.*

ANNE: Aye... aye... aye... aye... No... aye... aye... no... Like a scarecrow... *(She laughs)* Aye... Here she is. Aye, can't get out of her scratcher...

ALICIA: Who is it?

ANNE: Your pal, Kimberley.

ALICIA *grabs the telephone.*

ALICIA: Thank you, mother. I'll call you if I need you.

ANNE: I'll scream if I need you.

She exits USR

ALICIA *(deep breath)*: Never again. That's the second night running I've had the pants scared off me in my dreams.

Pause.

I know, but...

Pause.

If you suggest going down to the graveyard again you can count on me – not! It's the freakiest thing that's ever happened to me. There's no such thing as the living dead – when people die they're pure dead dead and that's an end to it.

Pause.

I can't talk here. My mum would kill me if she knew what I'd been up to.

Slight pause.

I'll see you at school.

Slight pause.

Okay. Bye!

She hangs up and lets herself fall back on the pillow. She sighs loudly.

ALICIA *(shouting)***:** Mother! More tea, darling!

> *Lights go down to blackout.*

SCENE THREE Playground Morning

In the darkness there are playground sounds. The lights come up. We find ALICIA, KIMBERLEY, BERNADETTE and SHAZ standing CS. They are dressed in coats, hats, and gloves. It is cold.

The sound fades to the background.

BERNADETTE: It's too early to be up. School should start at three o'clock in the afternoon.

KIMBERLEY: And finish at three-thirty.

ALICIA: So what's happening?

SHAZ: We've got to go back.

ALICIA: I know. We shouldn't have taken it.

SHAZ: I feel sick just thinking about.

BERNADETTE: I'm so frightened. I woke up with scratches on my feet.

KIMBERLEY: You should cut your toenails.

BERNADETTE: No, I mean serious scratches. I'm afraid to stretch out in bed. I've got to sleep curled up.

SHAZ: If we don't return the pendant I think we're going to hell. You know what we are? Graverobbers.

BERNADETTE: Don't say that. I didn't want to go. It was all of you. I said it was a stupid idea.

ALICIA: Stupid idea or not, we are where we are. So we've got to sort things out. Shaz's right. We've got to go back. Tonight.

KIMBERLEY: I can't tonight. I've got my dancing. It's the spring dance.

ALICIA: It's not spring yet.

SHAZ: It's the dance of death we'll be doing unless we sort all this out.

KIMBERLEY: Okay.

ALICIA: Just cancel it tonight, Kimberley. It'll all be over by tomorrow. Meanwhile, this is a secret. Nobody must know. Right, quiet. Here's the boys.

Enter THOMAS, ALI, DANIEL *and* DAVID.

THOMAS: What's the big secret, girls?

KIMBERLEY *(in one breath)*: There isn't a secret. Who said anything about secrets? I haven't said anything. I don't have any secrets, and even if I did, Alicia told me not to say anything. Particularly to you lot with your big gobs. *(Slight pause)* I'm sorry, girls, I think I've said too much.

THOMAS: So, Alicia, what's your secret?

ALICIA: I'll tell you later.

THOMAS: Later is ages away.

ALICIA: No it isn't, it's just like... *(She holds up her hand to snap her fingers.)*

Blackout.

SCENE FOUR Park Night

ALICIA, BERNADETTE, SHAZ, KIMBERLEY, THOMAS, ALI, DANIEL *and* DAVID *sitting on a park bench.*

ALICIA *has her hand up as she did at the last scene. She snaps her fingers.*

ALICIA: … that!

ALI: So, what's the story?

ALICIA: A few nights ago me and the girls broke into the graveyard.

THOMAS: Looking for a boyfriend?

The BOYS *laugh.*

ALICIA: You want to hear this or not?

THOMAS: Sorry. Go on.

ALICIA: It was just a laugh… or at least it was meant to be.

Lights go down slowly to blackout.

SCENE FIVE Graveyard Night

In the darkness we hear night sounds. The lights come up slowly.

ALICIA *and* BERNADETTE *enter from CSR. They are looking about.*

BERNADETTE: Where are they? We've been walking around for ages. This was a stupid idea. This place is creepy.

ALICIA: It's a graveyard. People get buried here. That's all. There's no such thing as ghosts or the undead or anything like that.

BERNADETTE: Aye, you keep telling yourself that. I once saw the ghost of my dead auntie.

ALICIA: Where did you see that?

BERNADETTE: In the toilet at school. In the mirror behind me.

ALICIA: It was probably Kimberley having a sly smoke.

BERNADETTE: Floating in the air?

> *KIMBERLEY and SHAZ enter from USC. They walk DS with their arms out like zombies. ALICIA and BERNADETTE turn and see them. They are terrified.*

KIMBERLEY and SHAZ *(together)*: We want life. Help us. We want life.

SHAZ: Too long in the cold ground.

KIMBERLEY: I want a… Kit-Kat!

> *SHAZ and KIMBERLEY start laughing.*

ALICIA: Very funny.

KIMBERLEY: You should have seen your faces!

ALICIA: I wasn't scared.

KIMBERLEY: Tell me about it.

SHAZ: Right, you two stop arguing. The plan was to walk from one end of the graveyard to the other. Where are we now?

BERNADETTE: Lost.

ALICIA: How can we get lost walking in a straight line? This is daft. Okay, which way do we go then?

> *They all look about.*

TOGETHER (all pointing in a different direction): That way!

ALICIA: Here, what's that? Over at that gravestone.

> *They walk USR.. A gravestone sits with a pendant hanging from it. BERNADETTE picks it up.*

BERNADETTE: Cool! Look what I've got.

GIRLS *(together)*: What is it? Let me see! We all found it! Halfers!

ALICIA: Let me see it, Bernadette. It looks like a pendant.

KIMBERLEY: Open it up. There might be a picture inside.

> *BERNADETTE hands the pendant to ALICIA.*

ALICIA: Right, don't all shove. I can't see what I'm doing. It's too dark.

KIMBERLEY is now walking around. She goes into her bag and pulls out a torch. She switches it on.

BERNADETTE: Open it, Alicia.

ALICIA: I'm trying Bernadette. It's stuck tight.

She manages to open the pendant.

SHAZ: Is it a picture?

ALICIA: No, it's words.

SHAZ: What's it say?

ALICIA *(reading)*: Be... a... It's no good. It's too dark.

They all turn to watch KIMBERLEY walking around with the torch.

ALICIA: Kimberley! What are you doing? Where did you get that torch?

KIMBERLEY: I always carry a torch. Doesn't everyone?

They all look at each other.

ALICIA: Well, no, actually. Never mind, bring it over here.

KIMBERLEY: I thought I heard something.

She crosses to USR and holds the torch in position

ALICIA *(reading)*: Beat... tender...

SHAZ: Beat tender? What does that mean?

ALICIA: Beat... tender... to join... us... That's it.

KIMBERLEY: It probably means hit the gravestone and the dead will rise.

BERNADETTE: I feel all cold. This is scary.

A movement in the curtains USC. BERNADETTE screams. They all scream and ALICIA drops the torch. They all run off DSR.

A wolf howls.

SCENE SIX Park Night

As Scene Four.

ALICIA: And that was it.

ALI: You still got it? The pendant? Where is it?

> ALICIA *takes the pendant from her pocket.* ALI *takes it and opens it.*

ALI: Must be worth a few bob.

> *The pendant is passed around the* BOYS *to look at.*

DANIEL: You going to sell it?

ALICIA: No, we're going to return it. We shouldn't have taken it.

BERNADETTE: I've been having scary dreams about it. It's like people or animals clawing at me. I've got scratches on my feet.

ALICIA: If I hear that story again!

DAVID: It's probably your cat.

> *The* BOYS *all laugh.*

BERNADETTE: I don't have a cat.

DAVID: You can have mine. It's going senile just now. Peeing all over the place.

BERNADETTE: I don't want a cat. I just want to return that pendant and get on with my life.

ALICIA: We didn't mean to take it. We just got scared and ran away.

DANIEL: What did you get scared of?

ALICIA: There were noises.

DAVID: Noises?

ALICIA: Anyway, we've all been having dreams. Funny dreams. So we're going back. And since you know about it you lot are coming with us.

ALI: Cool. When do we go?

ALICIA: Tonight. When everyone is asleep. Meet at the gates of the cemetery. I'd better get home now.

KIMBERLEY: If I'd known we were going that late I could have practised for my spring dance.

BERNADETTE: Come on, let's all go.

They all say goodnight, see you later, etc. and walk off in different directions.

SCENE SEVEN Bedroom Night

ALICIA *lies in her bed in the dark. The covers are up to her neck.*

ALICIA: I'm waiting here for everyone to go to bed. When you're waiting for something it always takes ages. Waiting for a party. Waiting for the weekend. Waiting for the end of a class in school. I seem to spend most of my time waiting. Hanging around and just waiting. I wonder, if you counted up all the time in a person's life that they spend waiting, would it add up to more than the time they spend doing things? That's funny if you think about it. Like funny strange.

MOTHER *(voice offstage)*: Alicia! Is that you talking to yourself again? They're going to cart you off if you keep that up! Go to sleep! Goodnight, love.

ALICIA: Goodnight, mum!

She pulls the cover off and stands up. She is fully dressed with a scarf tied around her neck.

Right, she'll be asleep in thirty seconds. I know how they are at that age. Imagine being thirty-one years old! Ancient. Right. Graveyard here I come.

She walks USR. She turns and looks at the audience.

The next bit probably isn't for those of a nervous disposition.

She exits.

SCENE EIGHT Graveyard Night

In the darkness we can hear the whispering of a lot of voices. We cannot hear what they say though. The voices are talking over each other, confused, meaningless. This should create a creepy atmosphere before the lights come up.

Lights come up to a moonlit night.

Figures are lying about the stage. It is the GHOULS from Scene One. They are lying down like bundles of rags. After a few seconds the 'rags' move. They rise up and come together CS. They go into a huddle and the whispering gets louder. It is deafening now. The GHOULS straighten up from the huddle. Still.

Silence.

They start to run about the stage as if they are looking for someone or something. After a few seconds of running around in silence the whispers grow again. The GHOULS go into their huddle again. They turn around and start pointing and screaming at the audience. Suddenly they stop dead and a silence falls like a knife. They all run off in different directions.

Pause.

From USC the GIRLS and BOYS enter. They all look terrified.

BERNADETTE: What was all that noise? What was that all about? I don't like it here. I want to go home. I'm tired. I'm really tired.

ALICIA: We're all tired, Bernadette. Just stop your whining.

KIMBERLEY: Look, there's the stone over there.

They all run USL to the gravestone.

ALI: Is this it. Come on put the pendant back and let's get out of here.

ALICIA takes out the pendant and places it over the stone.

ALICIA: Please let this be an end of it.

KIMBERLEY screams and points CSR. The GHOULS enter.

THOMAS: I feel sick.

DANIEL: This can't be real.

BERNADETTE *(screaming loudly)*: No!

The following sequence could be presented through a series of tableaux.

The GHOULS fight with the kids and grab BERNADETTE. She is dragged off CSR leaving everyone else lying dazed on the ground. They come to slowly.

ALICIA: Bernadette…? Bernadette…? What's happened?

KIMBERLEY: They took her. Those things dragged her away.

DAVID: I'm getting out of here.

They all agree.

ALICIA: What about Bernadette?

DANIEL: It's not our fault.

DAVID: Daniel's right. We're all scared. Let's just go home. If she's not back by the morning we can decide what to do.

ALICIA: Well, why not get help tonight?

DAVID: 'Cos if she turns up tomorrow all smiles then we've got ourselves in a lot of trouble for nothing.

DANIEL: David's right. Anyway, nobody forced Bernadette to come here. My dad's always saying that people have got to take responsibility for their own actions.

ALICIA: Well, I'll know what to do if you ever need help, Daniel.

KIMBERLEY: Alicia, I just want to get away from this. We're all tired and frightened. I'm not sure if what we think we saw is really what we saw. There might be a totally innocent explanation for all of this. Imagine we go back home screaming *ghouls*? People are going to think we're mad. How embarrassing is that? Tomorrow we'll see all of this a lot clearer. Although I think Daniel and David are scuzz bags, I think we should go. Alicia?

ALICIA: I think you're all wrong... but I'm not staying here by myself.

KIMBERLEY: Come on, let's go. We'll laugh about all of this tomorrow. And so will Bernadette.

They all exit USR.

Silence.

BERNADETTE (*voice offstage*): Please help me... please... I'm scared... Please somebody... help me...

A scream

Blackout.

SCENE NINE Bedroom Night

Darkness. A soft light comes up on ALICIA's bed. She is having a dream.

ANNE enters. It must be clear that she is part of the dream and not actually in ALICIA'S room. This can be done with lighting and her tone of voice. Music in the background can also create the right atmosphere.

ANNE: Have you done that homework?

ALICIA (*struggling*): I can't, mum, it's too difficult.

ANNE: Too difficult? For a bright girl like you?

ALICIA: It's the English homework...

ANNE: But of course it is... Remember what I told you...

> *She starts to walk out of the light, her voice getting quieter.*

Remember what I told you... Remember...

ALICIA wakes gasping for breath.

ALICIA: Mum? Oh no. Please, no. I know what it is. I understand. Oh, Bernadette, I understand.

> *The lights go down to blackout.*

SCENE TEN Playground Morning

In the darkness there are playground sounds. The light comes up to show all the children, apart from ALICIA, standing CS.

DAVID: I got this mad phone call from Alicia saying that she understood what happened.

KIMBERLEY: So did I.

They all nod their heads and agree.

DAVID: So what is there to understand?

SHAZ: Here she is now. Let's ask her.

ALICIA enters from USL.

So what's all this about, Alicia.

ALICIA: I had a dream last night and it was all explained to me. The answer was in our hands all the time. We shouldn't have gone back.

KIMBERLEY: You're telling us we shouldn't have gone back. The police are around at Bernadette's house right now and the head teacher is going to speak to us at assembly this morning.

ALICIA: Well, try and explain this. Do you know what an anagram is?

DAVID: It's something you get in English.

ALICIA: That's right. It's when you mix up the letters of a word and you get another word.

KIMBERLEY: What's that got to do with anything?

ALICIA: Listen, what did it say on the pendant?

KIMBERLEY: It said... Beat tender... to join us.

ALICIA: And what do you get when you mix up the letters of beat tender?

KIMBERLEY: Stop making a game of everything. What do you get?

ALICIA: You get Bernadette's name.

DANIEL: I don't understand.

ALICIA: Bernadette to join us.

KIMBERLEY: Oh my god...

ALICIA: They knew from the start. They always knew... From the beginning...

*The lights start to go down until there is just a spot on
ALICIA. The others leave the stage in silence.*

ALICIA: They used us... to bring Bernadette back... It was all planned...

A green light comes up softly to reveal BERNADETTE *standing
beside* ALICIA. *She is dressed like a* GHOUL. *When she
speaks her voice is very soft and low.*

ALICIA: It was like a dream...

BERNADETTE: Alicia... It's not your fault... It's not your fault... Alicia...

ALICIA: Bernadette... you're here... you're here and everything's all right now...

BERNADETTE: Of course it is... Everything is fine and I'm happy now... Come and join us...

ALICIA *falls to her knees slowly.*

The whispering that we heard earlier returns. It starts softly and grows louder.

ALICIA *screams as the lights go down to blackout.*

END OF PLAY

ACTIVITIES

Writing

Imagine you are the chief reporter for a local tabloid newspaper, *The Nightly Ghoul*. The readership of this newspaper is local ghouls and it hits the graveyards at night as soon as the sun goes down. Your job is to write a front page report on the incident described above.

Bear in mind that the audience of this report is ghouls! This affects how the incident is portrayed.

You will need to include the following: an account of the incident; an account of events leading up to it and anything relevant that has happened since (remember less than 24 hours have passed); details of people involved; eye-witness accounts; comment from sources and experts.

You also need to think about language and layout. Study real newspaper reports before you start to write. Think about this on your own or discuss these with your class: the headline; subheadings; columns; byline; structure of the report (for example, mentioning the most important information in the first one or two paragraphs); language features (such as the use of puns, sensational word choice, alliteration); attitude of the writer and angle taken in the article; how people and events are portrayed.

Media production

Produce the front page story describing Alicia's night of terror. Include:

- masthead (the newspaper's name)
- puffs (adverts)
- straplines (trailers for what is in the rest of the paper)
- the photograph (could be taken during tableau performance or sketched) and its caption
- headline and subheadings
- the report (laid out in columns)
- any other features you notice on front pages.

Scary moments – describing personal experience

Alicia and her friends probably learned a lot from their scary experience – although it doesn't look like they were going to live to tell anyone what it was!

1 Think about what the characters in *The Bone Orchard* learned and be prepared to talk about it in class.

2 Think about your own scariest moment. What did you learn about yourself and others? Did you change what you think or do because of it?

3 Describe your experience either in a solo talk to your class or an essay in your workbook. Suggest your feelings at the time through the way you describe what took place. If writing, try to create a sense of the atmosphere by using interesting describing words. If talking, create a sense of atmosphere by changing the pace, tone and pitch of your voice.

Anagrams

You learn from Alicia's mum, Anne, that an anagram is when 'you mix up the letters of a word to make another word'.

1 Below are some anagrams from *The Bone Orchard*. Work out the original words. If you are stuck, use the anagram clues – these give you a hint and the number of the page on which each anagram appears.

a) Slough   b) Dent pan   c) His glen

d) Hard cor   e) Seven go rat   f) Red ma

Anagram clues

a) You wouldn't want to meet this bunch of undead people in a graveyard in the middle of the night. (Page 72)

b) If only Bernadette hadn't picked this up from the gravestone… (Page 78)

c) The school subject which inflicted horrible anagrams on Alicia for homework. (Page 73)

d) A strange place to grow bones? (Page 71)

e) The pendant was found on one of these. (Page 78)

f) Alicia has a bad one at the start of the play. (Page 73)

2 Choose some other words from the play and make your own anagrams to test your classmates.